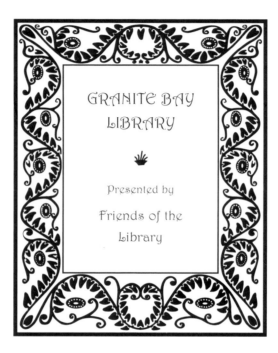

A BEACON BIOGRAPHY

MILLIE BOBBY BROWN

Nicole K. Orr

PURPLE TOAD
PUBLISHING

Printing   1   2   3   4   5   6   7   8   9

A Beacon Biography

Angelina Jolie	John Boyega
Anthony Davis	Kevin Durant
Big Time Rush	Lorde
Bill Nye	Malala
Cam Newton	Maria von Trapp
Carly Rae Jepsen	Markus "Notch" Persson, Creator of Minecraft
Carson Wentz	Millie Bobby Brown
Chadwick Boseman	Misty Copeland
Daisy Ridley	Mo'ne Davis
Drake	Muhammad Ali
Ed Sheeran	Neil deGrasse Tyson
Ellen DeGeneres	Peyton Manning
Elon Musk	Robert Griffin III (RG3)
Ezekiel Elliott	Stephen Colbert
Gal Gadot	Stephen Curry
Harry Styles of One Direction	Tom Holland
Jennifer Lawrence	Zendaya

Publisher's Cataloging-in-Publication Data
Orr, Nicole K.
    Millie Bobby Brown / written by Nicole K. Orr.
        p. cm.
Includes bibliographic references, glossary, and index.
ISBN 9781624693946
1. Actors—Spain—Biography—Juvenile literature. I. Series: Beacon biography.
 PN2287 2017
 791.45092

                                            Library of Congress Control Number: 2017956830

eBook ISBN: 9781624693953

ABOUT THE AUTHOR: Nicole K. Orr has been writing for as long as she's known how to hold a pen. She is the author of several other titles by Purple Toad Publishing and has won National Novel Writing Month eleven times. Orr lives in Portland, Oregon, and camps under the stars whenever she can. When she isn't writing, she is traveling the world or taking road trips. Why was this book perfect for Orr? Eleven happens to be her lucky number!

PUBLISHER'S NOTE: This story has not been authorized or endorsed by Millie Bobby Brown.

CONTENTS

Millie Bobby Brown and Finn Wolfhard were lucky to be at the 2017 San Diego Comic Con. The Duffer Brothers turned down hundreds of kid actors before choosing Millie and Finn to play Eleven and Mike.

"Stranger Things" Than First Kisses

Once upon a time, there was a high school in Indiana with monsters walking around outside. It was dark and scary and a very unusual place to have your first kiss. This was where the TV show *Stranger Things* filmed one of its last episodes, and it was here that the character Eleven had her first kiss. What most fans of the show might not know is that Millie Bobby Brown, who plays Eleven, had never been kissed before either.

Millie Bobby Brown wasn't the only one who was nervous about the scene. Finn Wolfhard, who played the co-kisser Mike Wheeler, was worried that his breath would smell bad. Just to be safe, Millie and Finn

The Duffer Brothers might be very popular at comic cons now, but their show **Stranger Things** *was actually turned down by more than 15 networks before Netflix made the right choice. Two years and 11 emmy nominations later, it looks like the Duffer Brothers were right!*

both ate an entire box of mints! Why was it especially difficult for them to stay in character? Their audience kept making them laugh!

Although the episode showed only four people in the scene, the classroom was crowded. The Duffer Brothers, the producers of *Stranger Things*, were there. The filming crew was there. Millie's father was there. Gaten Matarazzo (Dustin Henderson) and Caleb McLaughlin (Lucas Sinclair), the show's other two young main characters, could have gone home for the day. Their scenes had already been shot, but they were there too. They wanted to see the kissing scene! They stayed just outside the cameras' range and made funny, disgusted faces at Eleven and Mike.

The moment the kiss was over and the cameras were turned off, Millie shouted, "Kissing sucks!"

"Sorry!" Finn responded.[1]

It might not have been the most romantic place to have your first kiss, but Millie didn't mind. After all, this was show business.

While Millie hasn't had the chance to play a Disney princess yet, she does have little princess fans!

Millie at five years old singing the song "Valerie", and the area of Spain where she grew up.

Family Over Money

Born on February 19, 2004, in Málaga, Spain, Millie Bobby Brown loved the arts before she even knew what the arts were. As a kid, she had watched cartoons with her three siblings, Paige, Charley, and Ava. Using these cartoons, Millie taught herself an American accent. Next, she used musicals like *Chicago* and *Moulin Rouge* to learn how to sing. While her parents didn't start homeschooling her until she was older, Millie began homeschooling herself in the arts when she was still tiny.

When she turned four, Millie had her first chance to perform in front of an audience. She enrolled at the Pokesdown Community Primary School in Bournemouth, England. She was in many of their plays. When her family moved to Orlando, Florida, Millie was eight years old. Her parents, Robert and Kelly, were busy with their new teeth-whitening business, and Millie missed theater. Without it, she felt like a part of her was missing. She needed something to do, and her father found it for her.

Unlike Eleven's father in the series *Stranger Things*, Millie's real parents are very supportive. In fact, the whole Brown family is very close. Robert and Kelly Brown had noticed their daughter humming and dancing during cartoons when she was little. They wanted to help her follow those dreams, no matter how stressful or expensive that might become.

When Millie needed something to do to keep her busy, Robert enrolled her in a weekend stage school. Many of the arts were covered. There were classes in dancing, singing, and acting. It was there that Millie's talent was noticed outside the family. An agent saw her, liked her, and told her that she needed to live in California if she wanted to get the big roles.

At just twelve years old, Millie, with her family, moved to Los Angeles, California (L.A.). Within three months of arriving in L.A., Millie was cast as Alice in the TV series *Once Upon a Time in Wonderland*. When she was cast in the TV series *Intruders*, she had to act as if she were an adult trapped inside a ten-year-old's body. When the show's director Daniel Stamm was asked about Millie's performance, he said, "She has to say and do a lot of things that a ten-year-old girl wouldn't say and do."[1] As all of the directors and producers agreed, much of what she brought to the show was natural talent.

This natural talent helped her get cast in many small roles. These included parts on such TV series as *NCIS*, *Modern Family*, and *Grey's Anatomy*. She did commercials about pancakes and Barbie dolls. The problem was that she couldn't get any big roles. As time went on, she couldn't get the small ones anymore either.

Living in L.A. was expensive. It was even more expensive to make constant trips between the United States and the United Kingdom (U.K.). Millie said in an interview with the *Daily Mail*, "My older sister left. She didn't want to do it [America] anymore. It was tears, tears, tears. We went through tough times."[2]

Robert and Kelly Brown wanted Millie to follow her dreams, but what could they do when, in 2015, their money ran out? They all moved back to the U.K. Life was hard. Millie was beginning to think that she wasn't meant to be an actor. Maybe she should choose another dream. "I was devastated," Millie said in the interview with *The Daily Mail*[3] "I wasn't getting work. I thought I was done."

Millie had a conversation with a casting agent on the phone. The agent wasn't kind. She told Millie that she was TOO mature and TOO grown up. When Millie got off the phone, she was crying.

Millie had started out watching cartoons and using Disney to learn an American accent. Now she was told she seemed too old to act—Netflix was about to change her life.

Millie once interrupted an interview with GQ so she could show an editor some boxing moves.

3

The Price of Show Business

Sometimes the best things happen during the worst of times. This was the case with Millie Bobby Brown. In 2015, Millie had practically given up on acting. She and her family were living with an aunt in England. Millie was heartbroken, so when she got called in for one more audition that needed her to cry, it was easy to do. No one at the audition would tell her what kind of role it was. All she knew about the character was that she was named Eleven.

It didn't matter. The tears she shed at the audition were quite real, as were the shouts of success when she was told she got the role after four more auditions and a Skype chat with the producers.

Until this point, Millie's roles had been small. She'd played only small characters who didn't get many lines and weren't around for very long. When she was cast in *Stranger Things*, it quickly became clear that this role would be different. She was going to play the main character and have quite a lot of screen time.

Eleven might be a serious girl, but Millie likes to have fun. Once, she prank called her costume designer!

Stranger Things changed everything for Millie. Her days of being a small-time actress were behind her. Fast coming were the days when agents would fight to represent her, TV show hosts would overwhelm her with invitations, and she'd be auditioning for roles alongside the world's biggest stars.

While much about Millie's life changed after her big break, something about her appearance changed too. The producers of the TV series, the Duffer Brothers, didn't tell her she would need to shave her head until after she had been cast. Surprisingly, Millie's mother was more upset about her cutting her hair than Millie was. When Millie was interviewed by *SciFiNow*, she said, "I was like, 'Mum, let's just cut it off, it grows back, it's not permanent and I need to show how much

I'm involved with this character and how much I'm involved with the show." She went on to explain that there was another reason to shave her head. "Shaving my hair, it threw me off a little bit. I had quite long hair, but I thought, 'No, society's telling people that girls have long hair, boys have short hair.'"[1] Millie wanted to show girls and boys everywhere that their hair didn't matter. It didn't matter to Millie, it didn't matter to Eleven, and it shouldn't matter to the world.

As wonderful as getting her big break was, acting in *Stranger Things* was not easy. In 8 episodes, Millie's character Eleven had exactly 42 lines. While this was more than she'd had in anything else, it was an extremely small amount for a TV show's leading actor. Because she spoke so little, she was expected to say a lot in how she smiled, how she moved, or the look in her eyes. The acting was especially difficult in her very first scene on the set. Walking through the kitchen of a restaurant, she had to

Because of how many acting jobs she's getting now, Millie tells people she doesn't live in any one place. She lives on airplanes!

eat french fries that were cold and greasy. She had to eat three hamburgers that were terrible. She even had to eat her least favorite ice cream flavor: strawberry. The scene was a hard one to start with, but to Millie, it was a small price to pay.

Stranger Things is based in the 1980s, so Millie had to go through training. To teach her the right things to say and wear, the Duffer Brothers had her watch movies from the 1980s, such as *Stand By Me*, *The Goonies*, and *Poltergeist*. Most of all, it was the 1982 movie *E.T. the Extra-Terrestrial* that helped shape how Eleven would act. Millie pointed out that both *Stranger Things* and *E.T.* share a similar scene in which the main character is led around the house and taught about life.

When asked what she has in common with the character Eleven, Millie focused on protectiveness. Because of how close she is with her parents and her siblings, she has a drive to protect them. That was the emotion she used to make Eleven worry about and protect her friends. Another thing that Millie and Eleven have in common is their first kiss. When Eleven and Mike Wheeler kiss, it was the first time for both the super-powered character and for Millie.

When asked about one of the hardest scenes to film, Millie talked about one of the show's wetter moments. Eleven had to climb into a big tank of water, where she couldn't see or hear. She had to do it eight times to get the scene just right. As a girl who doesn't like small spaces, this wasn't fun. In order to make it easier, the Duffer Brothers would say things to make her laugh just before the cameras started. "I had this earpiece in and the Duffers, they're like my big brothers, and they would do noises," Millie said in an interview with *Click the City*. "They're like, 'Alright, everybody peed in the tank right after lunch, so basically you're swimming in pee.' " Millie said she responded to the joke with, "Lovely."[2]

When Ross Duffer told Millie she'd have to shave her head to play Eleven, he said to think of when actor Charlize Theron was in the movie Mad Max: Fury Road. *The actress shaved her head and ended up creating a memorable character.*

If Millie's family was worried that the excitement of acting would wear off, she soon put them at ease. On Millie's first day on the set of *Stranger Things*, she realized that she'd fallen in love with the right thing. She could no longer imagine life without acting. She even felt that if she were sick, all she would have to do is walk into her next acting job and she'd be healthy again. That was the power of acting to her. Now that she'd gotten a big role, she knew she was meant to be an actor.

The Duffer Brothers wondered if the young main actors of Stranger Things could be friends in real life and on the screen. If the actors performing the song "Uptown Funk" at the 68th Emmy Awards is anything to judge by, there's nothing to worry about!

Following Her
Other Dreams

After *Stranger Things* aired on Netflix, Millie might have thought life would get quieter. She'd have been wrong. Not only did kids everywhere dress up as Eleven for their 2016 Halloween costumes, but adults were getting tattoos of her face! It wasn't just Eleven who had a growing fan-base, however, but Millie herself.

In the twelve months following the release of the successful Netflix series, Millie was featured on *The Ellen DeGeneres Show*, *The Jonathan Ross Show*, and *The Tonight Show Starring Jimmy Fallon*. Plus, Millie was the youngest guest to appear on *The Late Show with Stephen Colbert*. In this last one, Millie said she would love to be Colbert's sidekick at the Emmys. While she didn't get to do that, she did help host other award shows. These included the Screen Actors Guild Awards, UNICEF's "youth takeover," the MTV Movie & TV Awards, and the Teen Choice Awards. Millie spent a lot of time at awards ceremonies. She wasn't just giving them out—she was also receiving them.

At the 2017 MTV Movie & TV Awards ceremony, Millie received the award for Best Actor in a Show. This award had never been given before. Why? In 2016, the complaint was made to MTV that there weren't any award categories that weren't based on gender. MTV was quick to respond by creating a new category that included men, women, and those who didn't label themselves as either one. Millie was proud of this change. After all, with her bald head, she'd been mistaken for a boy many times.

Millie was teary-eyed when she received her MTV Movie & TV Award, but she didn't get truly emotional until she met one of her biggest role models. Emma Watson, known for playing Hermione Granger in the Harry Potter movies, has been one of Millie's favorite actors her whole life. Fans of both women have pointed out how similar Emma Watson and Millie Bobby Brown look. Emma and Millie themselves are crossing their fingers that they get cast as sisters one day.

Once her dream of becoming an actor became reality, Millie had the chance to follow her other dreams. She'd loved musicals as a kid, so it was only natural for her to sing as an adult. Along with two of her *Stranger Things* costars, Millie performed the song "Uptown Funk" at the 2016 Emmys. Millie's YouTube channel shows videos of her singing at home, during interviews, and even while getting coffee. Proving how much she loves the music of Adele, Millie was in the drive-through lane at a Starbucks. Instead of letting her father simply order a latte and a caramel Frappachino, Millie leaned over and stuck her head out the window. She sang for her coffee in the style of Adele's song "Hello"—and did an amazing job!

Millie's love of music doesn't end with singing. In a surprising show of talent, she rapped Nicki Minaj's "Monster." She was also featured in a music video by Sigma. Lip-syncing and walking through a nighttime L.A., Millie looked as if she could have sung the song herself if she'd wanted to.

No matter how many famous people she meets on movie sets and in music videos, Millie never gets too shy to have a good time.

Despite how busy she has been, Millie continues to find time to have a roast dinner and movie with her family every Sunday. Whenever she wants to work off some of the stress from work, she uses her fists. She is a big fan of boxing and has a punching bag in her backyard.

There's no telling how long it might be until fans are forced to say goodbye to Eleven and the world of *Stranger Things*. However, when it comes to Millie Bobby Brown, she's already found several ways to take the show home with her. When she first saw a record player on the set of *Stranger Things*, she didn't know what it was. According to an interview with *The Vulture*, Millie turned to her father and asked, "What is that thing? It's like red and it's really weird and it's got a stick coming out of it and it's not right." Her father had her play something on it and it was love at first listen. Months later, her parents bought their daughter a record player for Christmas. She was very protective of it. When she came back from out of town and discovered her record player in her sister's room, she said, "Hey, you'd better give that back." Her sister replied, "I love it! It's amazing!" Millie didn't back down, saying, "I know, it's great. But it's mine."[1]

Something else Millie has taken away from the set of *Stranger Things* are her friendships. She constantly hangs out with her costars, and she has become best friends with co-star Winona Ryder. What do these two people have in common? Both of them started as very young

Millie and Winona Ryder stay great friends even away from the cameras. In fact, Millie often joins Winona for lunch and sometimes goes surfing with Winona's boyfriend.

When Stranger Things *won the Screen Actors Guild Award for Best Ensemble in a Drama Series, Millie did more than celebrate. She named her trophy Jeff.*

actors, and both had to shave their heads for their roles. Of course, their bond goes deeper than that. Millie thinks of Ryder as a mentor and a friend. At times, Ryder has come across like a mother to the four young main actors. During filming, Millie spent a lot of her free time in Ryder's trailer, sharing cheese and crackers.

While there might not be a way to predict how many seasons of *Stranger Things* there will be, fans of Millie can rest assured they will be seeing lots of her in the years to come. She has leapt into the world of acting, and she is most likely there to stay!

Millie is close to many of her costars, including David Harbor.

Making Friends

Millie Bobby Brown has a lot of fans, and a lot of them are stars themselves. Celebrities everywhere binge-watched the TV series and became eager to meet the actor behind Eleven. Among these have been actors Zac Efron, Lea Michele, and Sophia Bush. Maddie Ziegler, from the TV show *The Dance Moms*, has become best friends with Millie. Laverne Cox, an actor best known for the TV show *Orange Is the New Black*, was thrilled to meet her and the rest of the cast. She posted to her Instagram, "The highlight of the evening last night was meeting Millie, Gaten, and Caleb from 'Stranger Things.' These young people are both adorable and talented."

The actor Aaron Paul, best known for starring in *Breaking Bad*, is an especially big fan of Millie. He even said jokingly that he'd like to adopt her. According to an interview with *Click the City*, this was how Millie felt about the offer: "We said we'd go to lunch, he'd bring the adoption papers, I'll bring my suitcase, we'll make a deal." Apparently, even her parents felt comfortable with the arrangement. "My parents are like, 'Can we just have you on weekends?' "[1]

Despite how busy she is with *Stranger Things*, Millie still finds time to audition for other projects. She auditioned to be in the movie *Logan* as the second main character. Was she terrified of meeting an actor as famous as Hugh Jackman? Not only did Millie keep calm, but she ended up saying it was the best audition she'd ever done. Instead of being disappointed about not getting the part, Millie saw *Logan* and felt thrilled for Dafne Keen, the girl who got the role instead.

While most of her fans prefer to dress up as Eleven, many other kids dress up as Millie herself. Millie Bobby Brown has always had a good sense for clothes. And it isn't just fans who have noticed her style. In early 2017, the Calvin Klein Company hired her as a model for their new clothing line, Calvin Klein By Appointment. Only 15 models were chosen, and Millie was one of the lucky few.

Even though Millie was homeschooled for most of her childhood and then became an overnight star, she knows what it's like to be a regular kid. "I was seven when I was bullied by a boy," she explained in an interview with *The Wrap.* "No hard feelings, I got over it, but I did have to move schools because it was very hard, and I felt like I couldn't talk to anyone." She knew that there were other kids out there being bullied, both online and face-to-face. To fight against it, she created the Twitter account @Milliestophate. Most of her tweets are on stopping bullying, such as this one from July 26, 2017: "Be sure to taste your words before you spit them out." In the same interview, she explained the importance of her new Twitter account. "We need to stop bullying and cyberbullying. It's ruining people's lives."[2]

Millie spent a lot of time surrounded by monsters in *Stranger Things.* In 2017, she met one more monster when she was cast in *Godzilla: King of Monsters.* Very little was said about the plot or who else had been cast. Millie, however, started her research right away. When she got the part, she had never seen a Godzilla movie before. To prepare for her role, the actor Bryan Cranston invited her to watch the

2014 version of the movie. She's a lucky girl, as not everyone gets to see a Godzilla film with an actor who went up against the monster himself!

Godzilla might have a 2019 release date, but that doesn't mean Millie has stopped dreaming of bigger, better roles. When asked what TV show she'd most like to star in, she answered: *The Walking Dead*.

When it comes down to it, a Netflix monster, Godzilla, and even zombies aren't enough to scare Millie Bobby Brown. She might be terrified of sharks, but unless season two of *Stranger Things* features sharks making a snack out of Eleven, Millie is probably okay. After all, she's already had her first kiss on the show. What's more terrifying than that?

Millie will do almost anything for her fan base. Once she showed up to the 16th birthday party of one of her fans!

2004 Millie Bobby Brown is born in Málaga, Spain, on February 19.

2008 Millie enrolls at the Pokesdown Community Primary School in Bournemouth, England, the United Kingdom (UK).

2011 The Brown family moves to the United States, settling in Orlando, Florida.

2015 The Brown family runs out of money and moves back to the UK. Millie auditions for *Stranger Things*.

2016 Millie performs the song "Uptown Funk" with two costars at the Emmys.

2017 Millie receives an MTV Award for Best Actor in a Show. She auditions for the movie *Logan*. She is hired to model for the Calvin Klein Company. She is cast in *Godzilla: King of Monsters*. She is nominated for an Emmy for Best Supporting Actress in a Drama.

FILMOGRAPHY

2019 *Godzilla: King of Monsters* (Movie)

2016–17 *Stranger Things* (TV series)

2016 "Find Me" (Music video)

2015 *Modern Family* (TV series)

Grey's Anatomy (TV series)

2014 *Intruders* (TV series)

NCIS (TV series)

2013 *Once Upon a Time in Wonderland* (TV series)

Chapter One. "Stranger Things" Than First Kisses

1. Fallon, Jimmy. *The Tonight Show Starring Jimmy Fallon*: "The *Stranger Things* Kids Rehash That Kissing Scene." YouTube, September 1, 2016. https://www.youtube.com/watch?v=AQt9tM3fWsY

Chapter Two. Family Over Money

1. BBC America. *Inside Intruders: Meet the Incredible Millie Brown*. YouTube. September 3, 2014. https://www.youtube.com/watch?v=BUO1He3jgAQ

2. Graham, Caroline. "Defeated, Flat Broke." *Daily Mail*, August 2016.

3. Ibid.

Chapter Three. The Price of Show Business

1. Hatfull, Jonathan. "*Stranger Things*' Millie Bobby Brown on Playing Eleven." *SciFiNow*, July 21, 2016. https://www.scifinow.co.uk/interviews/stranger-things-millie-bobby-brown-on-playing-eleven/

2. Acosta, Beatriz. "Close Encounters with Eleven: Q&A with Netflix *Stranger Things* Star Millie Bobby Brown." *Click the City*, August 30, 2016. https://www.clickthecity.com/tv/a/30731/close-encounters-with-eleven-qa-with-netflix-stranger-things-star-millie-bobby-brown

Chapter Four. Following Her Other Dreams

1. Chaney, Jen. "*Stranger Things*' Millie Bobby Brown on Playing Eleven, Her Love-Hate Relationship with Scary Movies and Acting Without Speaking." *Vulture*, July 2016. http://www.vulture.com/2016/07/stranger-things-millie-bobby-brown-playing-eleven-scary-movies.html

Chapter Five. Making Friends

1. Acosta, Beatriz. "Close Encounters with Eleven: Q&A with Netflix *Stranger Things* Star Millie Bobby Brown." *Click the City*, August 30, 2016. https://www.clickthecity.com/tv/a/30731/close-encounters-with-eleven-qa-with-netflix-stranger-things-star-millie-bobby-brown

2. Welk, Brian. "Millie Bobby Brown Opens Up in Her Fight Against Bullying." *The Wrap*, July 29, 2017. http://www.thewrap.com/millie-bobby-brown-opens-up-in-her-fight-against-bullying/

Books

Adams, Guy. *Notes from the Upside Down: An Unofficial Guide to* Stranger Things. New York: Touchstone, 2017.

Wizards RPG Team. *Dungeons and Dragons Starter Set.* Renton, WA: Wizards of the Coast, 2014.

Works Consulted

Bayley, Leanne. "21 Facts About Millie Bobby Brown from *Stranger Things.*" *Glamour*, August 14, 2017. http://www.glamourmagazine.co.uk/gallery/millie-bobby-brown-facts-age-parents-interview-bio

Gavilanes, Grace. "10 Celebs Who Are Proud Members of the Millie Bobby Brown Fan Club." *People*, August 28, 2017. http://people.com/tv/6-celebs-who-are-proud-members-of-the-millie-bobby-brown-fan-club/

Hirschberg, Lynn. "Millie Bobby Brown on the Aftermath of *Stranger Things*: 'My Whole Life Changed.' " *W Magazine*, June 29, 2017. https://www.wmagazine.com/story/millie-bobby-brown-stranger-things-godzilla

Lawrence, Derek. "Emma Watson and Millie Bobby Brown Met at MTV Movie and TV Awards, and It Was Adorable." *Entertainment*, May 7, 2017. http://ew.com/tv/2017/05/07/mtv-movie-tv-awards-millie-bobby-brown-emma-watson-hugh-jackman/

Robson, Shannon Vestal. "She's Only 13, but Millie Bobby Brown Is Already Cooler than Most of Us." *Pop Sugar*, May 9 2017. https://www.popsugar.com/celebrity/Millie-Bobby-Brown-Facts-43514712

Rubin, Rebecca. "Millie Bobby Brown Reveals She Auditioned for *Logan* with Hugh Jackman." *Variety*, May 30, 2017. http://variety.com/2017/film/news/millie-bobby-brown-logan-audition-1202437844/

Ryle, Adela. "21 Essential Facts About Netflix Retro-Fest Thriller *Stranger Things* Star Millie Bobby Brown." *Mirror*, July 29 2016. http://www.mirror.co.uk/tv/21-essential-facts-netflix-retro-8522709

Vincent, Alice. "Eleven Out of 10: How *Stranger Things* Star Millie Bobby Brown Charmed the World." *The Telegraph*, September 24, 2016. http://www.telegraph.co.uk/on-demand/2016/09/24/eleven-out-of-10-how-stranger-things-star-millie-bobby-brown-cha/

On the Internet

Facebook: Millie Bobby Brown
https://www.facebook.com/milliebobbybrown/

Internet Movie Database: "Millie Bobby Brown"
http://www.imdb.com/name/nm5611121/

YouTube: Millie Bobby Brown Central
https://www.youtube.com/channel/UCgCwRw_sls9RREurCRQGUKA

audience (AW-dee-untz)—The people who watch a show.

binge-watch (BINJ-watch)—To watch a lot of episodes of the same show, one right after another.

devastated (DEH-vuh-stay-ted)—Extremely sad and upset.

earpiece (EER-pees)—A tiny speaker that is worn inside the ear so that people can talk to the wearer from a distance without others hearing.

homeschool (HOHM-skool)—To educate or learn at home instead of in a school.

lip-sync (LIP-sink)—To mouth the words to a song in perfect time.

mentor (MEN-tor)—An unofficial teacher.

permanent (PER-muh-nent)—Lasting until the end.

rap—A style of music in which words are mostly spoken, not sung.

record player (REH-kurd PLAY-er)—A machine that plays music recorded on a flat vinyl disk (called a record).

Skype (SKYP)—A computer program that allows people to talk to one another, with a video option to also view one another at the same time.